The Karate Guy

By

Jeffery C. Washington

Dedication

This book is dedicated to my wonderful family. I would like to thank you all for your support and encouragement. To my karate teachers that I learned from. The classmates, and competitors I have trained with and fought against over the years. I thank you all for helping me become who I am today. I love you all.

Karate

When people think about karate, they imagine seeing tough guys, like Bruce Lee or Chuck Norris, doing spinning kicks and back flips, breaking things, yelling, and beating bad guys up. Everybody who has started taking martial arts doesn't know what they are getting into, and they will probably have many wild experiences. But for whatever reason, they begin with self-defense, exercise, discipline, or plain curiosity. One thing is for sure, they will learn a lot about themselves.

Who am I?

I grew up in Harrisburg, a small town in Pennsylvania, where the winters were cold and snowy, the fall was brisk and windy, the spring was cool and wet, and the summers were hot and dry. People in our small town had the pleasure of enjoying all four seasons. Still, I loved the summer, people washing their cars, painting their houses, and, oh yeah, the girls wearing fewer clothes. Still, the main reason I enjoyed the summer was because school was out, which is one of the best experiences for a kid anyway, besides Christmas or your birthday, which also happened in the summer for me.

My birthday was four days after school let out. I remember this particular summer; I was celebrating my tenth birthday with my family. My mother, Lynn, my father, Ron, my older

Sister Patty and my older brother, Ron Junior. My brother and sister were both in high school. I didn't see them much because they both stayed at their friends' houses across town. Today, that didn't matter; they were home celebrating my birthday, and they brought me presents. I felt special. Also at the party were my Uncle Marvin and my Aunt Wanda; they came to my birthday party every year and always gave me great presents and some money. I knew it was a good party because all I heard from my dad was.

"We're spoiling the boy," that was his way of saying, Jeff, make sure you say thank you for everything.

Things were going great, and then I opened a present that made me feel like I had died and gone to heaven. It was the one from my uncle Marvin, a professional Spalding basketball.

As soon as I saw it, all the other presents didn't matter. I pictured myself slam dunking at the corner playground basketball court. I couldn't wait to play, so I asked my mom,

"Can I go play?"

Even though the party wasn't over, my mother reluctantly said,

"Go ahead, Jeff," so I grabbed the ball and went to the playground.

My buddy Greg lived down the street between my house and the playground, so I had to pick him up on the way.

There were a few reasons why I liked Greg, one was because we were about the same size, short for our age, and another reason was when we played games together, sometimes I won and sometimes he won, even though I won the most, he didn't care. Greg was a good loser, so we very rarely fought while playing games. It was always a good competition.

Greg would have been at my birthday party, but my mother told us it was for family only, so that's another reason I wanted to leave the party. I knew Greg would be waiting for me, and just as I thought Greg was sitting on his porch steps, as Greg saw me dribbling the ball down the street, he immediately yelled,

"First outs!" I said,

"You got it," and I threw him the ball. Greg looked at the ball and said enviously,

"This is a real ball." I smiled and said,

"You know it." Greg and I were such good friends he felt like my ball was his too, so away we went to the basketball court. When we got there, we were in luck, the courts were clear. Two guys, a good basketball, a free court, and a warm summer day man for a ten-year-old, you couldn't ask for anything better.

So we started playing ball, and that's when it happened, before I made my first shot, my great day was over. The big boys showed up, forty or fifty of them, yelling and cussing, the usual thing,

"Clear the court you little scrubs!"

It really was only four big guys, but it felt like forty or fifty, and they were cursing at me. It was Lenny, Bobby, Ty, and Black. They were kind of like playground bullies. They were fourteen and famous for starting trouble, but they usually didn't mess with me unless they saw me. So I tried to stay out of sight, but this time, they were interrupting my wonderful day, and I was mad about them calling me a scrub, so I yelled back,

"No, we aren't going nowhere, we were here first!" they walked right up to me and said,

"We?" I answered back,

"Yes we!" Then I looked around, and Greg was gone, I was alone. I felt surprised, embarrassed, scared, and a couple of other emotions I just didn't come to grips with at the time. I wanted to argue my case with them, but they weren't the kind of guys that cared about your case, so even though I was mad, I was not stupid. So I picked up my ball and started walking away. And that's when it started getting crazy, Lenny yelled,

"Hey punk, where are you going with my ball?" I immediately said,

"This is my ball," then they surrounded me, talking to each other. Bobby said,

"Lenny, are you going to let this punk walk off with your ball?" I repeated myself again,

"This is my ball!" They continued talking and laughing to each other, and then Bobby said,

"Give him a choice, man." Lenny smiled and said,

"OK, little man, I am going to give you a choice, you either give me my ball, or I'll kick your butt and take your ball, your choice."

Ty and Black both laughed. I didn't like either of those choices, so even though I was correct, their numbers and size made me realize they wouldn't listen to a third choice. I took my ball and left the court, so sadly, I gave them my brand-new professional Spalding basketball.

I don't know what felt worse, giving those butt holes my ball, or listening to them laugh at me as I walked away from the playground.

About a block from the playground, there was a small dirt lot, that's where I met up with Greg. I asked with confusion,

"What happened to you?" Greg responded concerned,

"What happened to you?" I replied,

"Thanks a lot, they took my ball," Greg said, humbled,

"Man, when I saw Lenny, I knew it was time for me to go, besides, you're always bragging about how good you can fight, I thought you could handle it."

Greg was right, I bragged a lot about how I could fight, the truth was, I had never been in a real fight before. My brother told me one of his strategies which was to act as if you can fight, talk like you can fight, and it will make guys leave you alone.

It does work on most guys, but some guys like to fight. In those cases you have to fight to prove you are better than them. I never thought I would have to prove it to guys bigger than me. So I replied like an ordinary ten-year boy,

"I can fight, I just choose to pick my battles,"

Greg answered back,

"You know the only picking in that battle would be, you picking your butt off the ground after he knocked you out. As long as I have known you, I have never seen you fight anybody." I started walking towards Greg and said,

"I know I can kick your butt." Greg straightened up and said,

"Bring it," and then we started wrestling, but because I wasn't mad at Greg, the wrestling match turned into a game. I yelled,

"I'm Hulk Hogan!" Greg yelled,

"I'm the super fly Jimmy Snuka," and we played wrestling till we got tired. We then sat and rested. Greg said,

"You know what we need to do," I asked skeptically,

"What?" Greg answered,

"We need to learn karate!" I said,

"How are we going to learn karate?" Greg said,

"I saw Chuck last week, and he was wearing this white suit, so I asked him why he was wearing a white suit, and he said he was taking karate over at the hill action center, we should go!"

Chuck was also ten, but he was bigger than Greg and me, and even though I was a little scared, that might be a way to get my ball back. So why not try it? I knew I would need some help, yeah, karate, I think after a week of karate, I'll get my ball back, and then again, Lenny is kind of big, maybe two weeks.

I always hear so much about karate and never miss the TV show Kung Fu. I was extremely interested, so I said to Greg,

"Let's go to chuck's house," Greg said,

"OK," so off we went.

Chuck lived about two blocks up from us, and it had to be important for ten-year-old boys to walk two blocks in the summertime. When we got to Chuck's house, we were in luck. Chuck was just on his way to karate class. We knew that because he was wearing a pair of white pajamas, and around his waist, he was wearing a thick white belt tied up with a knot in the front. It had two green stripes at the end; he was going either to karate or bed. When Greg and I first saw Chuck, we laughed, and even though Chuck looked silly, I wished I had some white pajamas, too. Greg and I both said at the same time,

"Are you going to karate?" Chuck answered,

"Haee!" we both said, puzzled,

"What?" Chuck answered,

"Haee means yes in Japanese, that's what we say at the dojo." Greg and I didn't know what he was talking about, so I asked,

"What is a Doe Joe?" Chuck answered,

"That's also Japanese, that means the place you practice Karate."

It did sound kind of weird, but at the same time, it sounded cool. I then asked,

"Chuck can we take karate?" He answered,

"Sure it's a buck a lesson." Greg hung his head down and said,

"I don't have any money," I said to Greg,

"I got you, man," it was my birthday, and I was loaded. I had five bucks. I wanted Greg to come, he was my buddy. I wanted somebody there I knew I could beat. So Chuck, Greg, and I went downtown to the Hill Action Center to get my ball back, excuse me, I mean, to learn karate.

On the way, we saw another guy with white pajamas, but he had long hair. As we got closer, we discovered that he was, in fact, she. It was the girl who lives next door to me. I didn't know what surprised me more, that she was taking karate or that I didn't even know her name. I was ten years old and had just started getting into girls. I thought I was supposed to know all of them, but just then, Chuck yelled,

"Konee Chee wha, Venus!" she yelled back,

"Konee Chee wha, Chuck!" they walked up and looked at each other, then bowed like they were going to hit their heads together. Greg and I looked at each other and started to laugh. Chuck said,

"If you are going to take karate, you better get used to this," the girl said,

"Yeah, or you better get used to a lot of pushups," Chuck and the girl looked at each other and laughed. Chuck then introduced us,

"Jeff and Greg, this is Venus,"

"Venus this is Jeff and Greg." Venus, so that's her name. Chuck continued,

"Venus, Jeff, and Greg are going to start taking karate today, "Venus said, rubbing her hands together,

"Good, fresh meat." Usually, if a guy had said that I would have been nervous, but I wasn't going to let her worry me. Besides, I was on a mission to get my professional Spalding basketball back.

When we got to the center, a man was at the door. He was old, had gray hair and wrinkles, and was very friendly. Chuck and Venus told him, Mr. Dorsey, this is Jeff and Greg. They're going to start taking karate today. The man said,

"Two more soldiers for our family's army, that will be a dollar each." We paid him our money and went inside. Chuck and Venus told Greg and I to take off our shoes. Then they advised us that we had to bow our heads to the room before we could enter the doe joe.

I thought that was a little strange, but I didn't care. I had a ball out there somewhere, and I wanted it back, and if I had to take off my shoes and bow my head to get it, I was going to do it.

We walked into a large room with no furniture. It had a wooden floor like an indoor basketball court, but there were no lines. There were about six other kids standing around. The first thing I noticed was that some of the kids didn't have white pajamas, so that made me feel a little better. Chuck and Venus told Greg and me that the teacher would be out in a few minutes. They said the teacher was giving a karate test in the next room.

All of a sudden, we heard a loud crash. (Boom) Suddenly, a hole appeared in the wall in the front of the room, and in the hole, a man's arm, shoulder, and head were sticking out. As suddenly as it appeared, it disappeared. Greg and I stood there with our eyes bugged out, and our mouths wide open. The other kids acted like nothing had happened, and I started getting nervous.

About a minute later, four men entered the room; two had brown belts on, and two had black belts on. I started thinking who are these guys? I didn't know these were some of the best karate men in the city.

One of the men wearing a brown belt was tall and thin. I think I'll call him slim; the other brown belt was a bit fat; yeah, I'll call him fatty. Just then, someone yelled,

"Kee at sue kay!" I found out later, which meant get lined up.

Everybody started running to get in line. Chuck grabbed me and Greg, and put us up in front of the class, and said,

"Just do what everybody else does."

All of my life, I was the kind of kid who did what he wanted to do. To say it straight, I was a bit of a brat. When the teacher started talking I knew I better listen. He said,

"All right, we got a lot of work to do today, so let's get started." The class yelled,

"Yes, sain say," which meant yes, teacher. Even though everybody else was quiet, I felt I needed to ask a question, so I raised my hand and said,

"Work? What work?" at that time, I didn't know what was so funny, but the brown belts and one of the black belts just started smiling. The headteacher didn't flinch, but the two brown belts ran up to me, stood in my face, and yelled,

"Did anybody ask you to talk, boy!" I almost pooped my paints. I realized that maybe I shouldn't have asked that question, so I answered nervously,

"No," then fatty said,

"Do I look like a little boy to you!" I again responded nervously,

"No." Then Slim yelled,

"Then you better put a sir behind that NO, boy!" I don't know if it was that they were bigger than me or that they had the worst breath I have ever smelled in my life, but I could tell they meant business. Then Slim said,

"Drop and give me twenty," I asked nervously,

"Twenty what?" then the whole class started giggling, and Slim and Fatty both yelled,

"Twenty pushups boy!!"

So this is what they meant by getting used to doing pushups. Even though I didn't know if I could even do twenty pushups, I got down and started doing pushups, and that's how I got formally introduced to karate. After I got up the teachers yelled at us for two hours,

"Punch, Block, Kick, Pushup, Sit-up, Jump, Get Down." I got worked out. When class was over, I was beat. Greg, Chuck and I were walking home, and Greg said,

"This karate stuff is not easy." Chuck said, "Yeah," then I said,

"Yeah, Greg, if it were easy, everybody would know karate." I thought to myself, *wait till Lenny finds out I know karate, he'll be sorry.* I asked Chuck,

"By the way, what does Sain say mean?" Chuck answered,

"It means teacher in Japanese, and you spell it, S, E, N, S, E, I, don't forget it." Right then I knew I had a lot to learn. The first thing I had to learn was the names of the black and brown belts that taught us in class.

The brown belts that tormented us that first day continued to do so as often as possible. The one I had named Slim was named Mac, and he obviously liked his name because he had it stitched all over his karate uniform. If that wasn't enough, he had Mac attack tattooed on his chest and down his arm. Yes, Mac loved his name.

Fatty's name was Reggie. His job was to bust people's balls twenty-four hours a day, seven days a week. I always pictured Reggie at his house telling everybody in his family to drop and give him twenty. Even though they were not the friendliest guys, there were good at karate. Man, they could kick so fast and high and punch really hard too.

I loved seeing them fight, they always put on a show. They were so good because they were taught by two of the toughest black belts in the city, or maybe the state. Let's face it, the way I saw it, they were the best in the world!

My first teacher was Sensei Walt. He stood about six foot two, had a stocky build, and looked cool as hell with his goatee. When I grow up, I'm going to grow a goatee.

And then there was his teacher, master instructor Sensei Lee; he was stocky as well, with a bald head, and he had two of the most enormous hands I have ever seen on a human being. He was as tough as he was smart.

Greg and I went to karate class for about a week, and even though it was tough, I was determined to learn how to get my ball back. One day, I went to get Greg for class, and he was sitting on his porch. I said,

"Hey man, you ready to go?" He answered,

"I'm done man," I asked, concerned,

"What do you mean, you're done?" He replied,

"Karate is too tough, my arms are killing me, and I can hardly feel my legs, like I said, man I'm done," I thought to myself. *What a wimp.* I told Greg,

"Whatever, man, I'm gone."

So, I went to karate class for the first time without my buddy. Greg was right, karate was hard, but I was determined to continue. I know not having Greg in karate class would concern me because he helped me learn some things. He also took some of the heat off of me, so I knew I would miss having him in class, but I didn't care. I had a mission to get my ball.

Do I know what I want?

Three weeks later, I was getting very discouraged. I practiced karate for about a month, and I only learned how to clean the dojo floor and do pushups. It was funny. The best way I could explain it was each day, I was compelled to keep going because I knew karate was more than just cleaning the dojo. Besides, no basketball is worth this much.

The next class felt the same. The only difference was that Sensei Lee was teaching the class alone because the other higher-ranked belts were doing a karate demonstration across town.

Class started as usual, but then something happened that blew my mind. Two threatening guys came to the center. One was tall, about six foot five, and burly, with a mustache covering his top lip. The other was five foot eleven and obese, with poppy eyes and big lips, and they both were terrifying. They were yelling crazy stuff at the top of their lungs,

"Karate ain't nothing, we'll kick all your butts." They walked right up to the front of the class, and then they made the mistake of getting right up in Sensei Lee's face, and they yelled,

"You're not so tough without your partner!" Sensei Lee did not even flinch. His confidence surprised them. They thought they had a good plan. The two idiots waited outside till they saw Sensei Walt and the other higher-ranked belts leave the center, and then they decided to come in. They wanted to outnumber Sensei Lee, but what the two ruffians didn't know was that Sensei Lee was brilliant, he looked at the two guys and asked,

"Do you want to fight me in front of all these little kids?"

The two guys turned their heads and looked at the kids in the class. Turning their heads was like pushing a button in Sensei Lee's mind. Like a cat, he leapt into action. Sensei Lee suddenly stepped to the side, and with one punch, he delivered a perfect blow to the tall guy's head. His eyes immediately shut, and almost at the same time, Sensei Lee's leg flew up in the air and landed on the fat guy's shoulder. The techniques were so quick and precise that the two guys dropped to their knees almost at the same time. I had never seen anything as cool as that, not even on TV. It seemed like a wild, choreographed dance. I have heard many stories about Sensei Lee, but seeing the story unfold in front of your eyes is amazing. Sensei Lee knew they had enough, so he then said to the beaten individuals smugly,

"You two guys got your first lesson for free. The next one will be a dollar each." Then he grabbed them both by the hair and dragged them both outside the center at the same time and told them,

"Have a good day." The other students and I knew we had witnessed an incredible feat. Still, Sensei Lee acted like nothing had happened. I was blown away. Sensei Lee addressed the class and said,

"I can teach you many karate techniques, but I can't teach you when to use those karate techniques. That's your job to learn when to use the techniques."

That lesson gave me a brilliant idea. I decided to ask Sensei Lee to help me get my ball back. I'd love to see Lenny and Bobby give Sensei Lee the choice they gave me. This was great. My own Chinese connection. As soon as class ended, I ran up to Sensei Lee and told him the whole story about my basketball, and then I got brave. I asked him,

"Can you get my ball back?" Sensei Lee touched his chin and said,

"Hmmm, let me see. Do you want me to get your ball back?" I said excitedly,

"Yes!" He said,

"How?" Still excited, I said,

"You can kick Lenny in the head and punch Bobby in the eye, and if you want, you can smack Ty and Black just for fun. I know you can do it without even breaking a sweat." Sensei Lee smiled and said,

"I see, Jeff, but what if I could show you how you can get your ball back, all by yourself?" I smiled and said,

"Good, are you going to hold Lenny, at the same time, I kick his butt?" Sensei Lee laughed and said,

"Yeah, we'll make that plan B, just tell me where Lenny lives." I told him where Lenny lived and he shocked me and said,

"Let's go."

"Right now?" I asked. He nodded and said,

"No time better than the present."

I couldn't dispute that wisdom, so off we went. Usually, I would have been scared, but I was with Sensei Lee. I just knew I was protected.

The walk seemed to last forever. We didn't say much to each other, so I wasn't sure what the plan was. I was with my new secret weapon, so that calmed me as we came closer to Lenny's house. I saw Lenny in front of his porch, and can you believe it, he was playing with my ball. I started getting sick, but Sensei Lee's confidence made me feel better.

We walked up to Lenny, and then Sensei Lee said to me,

"Ask for his mother."

I said to Lenny, in a quiet scared voice, "Is your mom home?" Lenny said,

"Who wants to know?"

Sensei Lee pushed me aside and said,

"We want to know." When Lenny saw Sensei Lee, he got scared and ran into the house yelling,

"Mom" I never thought I would ever be at Lenny's house. I never saw Lenny scared, so I was amazed, and then Lenny's mom walked out. She asked with a concerned look,

"What's the matter?" Sensei Lee looked at me and said,

"Tell her." I was scared because Lenny was standing right there in front of me, so I just blurted it out,

"Lenny took my ball." Lenny's mom said,

"I wondered where that ball came from. Lenny give that boy his ball." I was a little surprised at how easy it was and said,

"Thank you." Sensei Lee also said thank you, and we turned and walked away. At last is was over, all the weeks of practice, all the pain, and suffering. It was settled by me just asking for my ball. But at that particular point, I didn't care. I had my ball back, and nobody even lifted a finger.

Still, somehow, I felt a little different, it seemed as if something was missing as Sensei Lee, and I were walking away. I had to say,

"Sensei, you didn't even think about it today in class. You just kicked butt, now, no kicking, no punching, no butt-kicking." Sensei Lee replied,

"Yes, that's correct." I thought for a minute then asked,

"What will stop Lenny, or anybody else, from retaking my ball?"

Then Sensei said something that changed my life forever, he said,

"Lenny is about fifteen years old. If you fight him and lose, he will keep on bullying you. If you fight him and beat him, you would embarrass him, and that would make him mad at you for a long time, and maybe he would even try to get revenge. Then you'll have to keep on fighting. Now he is mad at me and his mom. Adults always tell kids to do something they don't want to do. He'll get over that. For now, the fighting is over. Just be glad for that.

Today in class, I had to protect myself. Those guys who came into the dojo didn't want to talk, they wanted to fight. I had no choice but to give them what they wanted. Keep coming to karate class to learn when to negotiate or delegate. It could save your life." That's when I began to understand what he was trying to teach us. They weren't just teaching fighting skills and techniques. They were teaching us how to know when or if to fight.

The Karate Game of Tag

Three months passed, the wind blew more, and the leaves on the trees started changing from green to various shades of yellow, red, and orange. I didn't mind the fall much. It made things feel different. The folks were tired of doing yard work. People were complaining about how short their vacations were, and the ladies started putting on more clothes. I was still going to karate class. I even got my white pajamas, also known as a Gi. Having my karate uniform made me feel like I fit in. The students began to treat me differently too. They stopped calling me fresh meat, and after a few sparring sessions, it seemed as if some of them feared me.

But not the brown belts. They still treated me like dirt, and the black belts never stopped amazing me. I saw then punch, kick through boards, and break red bricks with their bare hands and feet. It helped me realize how much I didn't know. Man it was hard. I don't understand why they called it practice, it seemed more like torture with exercise. I remember doing arm blocks till my whole arm was black and blue. Kicking for hours till my legs felt like jelly, all those pushups on my knuckles, and after all that, those pushy teachers yelling,

"Do more!"

Training seemed endless. I remember Sensei Walt's famous quote was,

"Our arms, hands, legs, and feet must prepare to become weapons. You don't want your weapon to break in the middle of a fight, so sharpen it well. If you practice inferiority, you will perform inferiority, which could be the difference between life and death." He always made everything seem so terrifying.

Because I was so new, I rarely got a chance to spar with higher-ranking students. So instead I mostly did kata exercises, what I hit most was air. Then, one day, Sensei Lee came to the kids' class and said,

"We are going to spar. There's going to be a tournament coming up, and I would like for all of you to compete." Everybody yelled,

"Me!" so I yelled,

"Me too!"

Chuck and Venus were jumping up and down, saying,

"I can't wait to get to the tournament," even though I did yell, I didn't really know what a karate tournament was, so I waited a while and pulled Chuck aside and asked,

"What's a karate tournament?" Chuck explained,

"That's where we go to another town and spar against other karate schools. You know how sensei always says in class hold back? At the tournament, you don't have to hold back. It's either kick butt or get your butt kicked." All right, this is what sensei meant, learn to fight or when to negotiate. I could hardly wait.

Sensei Lee cared about us. He didn't want us to lose because he thought we might lose confidence in ourselves if we lost at the tournament. So, in the following weeks, classes became extraordinarily complex. Sensei Lee and the other instructors taught us the karate tournament rules: Rule number one, no deliberate contact to the face or groin. Even though I was ready to fight, I liked that rule.

Rule number two was no turning your back. That means you can't run away, and there were at least ten more. Oh well, all I know is that what the tournament rules meant wasn't the only thing Sensei taught us. We also worked on special tournament techniques to improve our stamina. Sensei Lee wanted us to be ready for anything, and to perform as long as we could.

Throughout all the training of kicks, punches, and blocking, the thing I liked the best was sensei always stressed to us that our school was a family. We should always keep our heads up and have pride in ourselves and our school. All he wanted was for the contestants to do their best. Winning or losing didn't matter.

Weeks of practice went fast and before we knew it we were in our last practice before the tournament. It was very weird for me since this would be my first one and I didn't know what to expect.

All the other kids in the class were getting nervous, but not me. I was getting excited. It was like I was going to my birthday party, and I knew they were going to have my favorite flavor of ice cream. That's the best way I could describe it. Sensei Lee stood up in front of the class and said,

"I have trained you, and you have learned a lot, now it is time for you to show me if our karate is beneficial, but even more important than that, to also show you that you are human, and that you can win or lose, you should except your wins the same as your losses."

After class, Chuck and I were walking home, and he said,

"Man even thought I have been in several of these tournaments, I still get nervous,"

"Why is that?" I asked.

Chuck replied,

"You're in a lower ranking division than me. The guys in my division don't play. The last tournament I went to, I saw a guy get his nose broken, blood was everywhere." Even though I was confident, I didn't need to hear that. When we got to Chucks' house, he started to go in, but he stopped and looked back at me, and said,

"Jeff, this is your first tournament, it's my third, don't worry about it, just fight like you do in the dojo, and you'll be cool."

You know, when someone tells you not to worry, you always start worrying for some reason. That night, lying in bed, I started going through all my karate techniques in my head. I thought to myself, I have to win, but then I remembered what sensei said, "Just do your best." I think that's the only thing that helped me go to sleep.

The next morning, it was a bright and sunny fall day. Even though it was cool outside, I was ready to rumble, so I grabbed my uniform and ran to the center to get a ride to the tournament. I was the first one there, and just then, I saw a big van coming up the street. It was Sensei, Walt. He yelled,

Get in and move to the back."

Soon after that, the others arrived, and we took off. We drove for several hours. I thought it would take forever to get there. Then I heard one of the other kids yell,

"There it is!" Yes, there it was, a big gray building with large windows in front and a big parking lot on the side. People were everywhere, and most were wearing karate uniforms, all walking to the front of the building. Sensei Lee said,

"Ok guys, get in a line and lets go in." When we got into the building, I didn't know what to expect. The first thing I saw was a big gym with eight big squares made out of tape on the floor. Everyone called them rings, and I thought rings were supposed to be round. Sensei yelled,

"Go get ready!"

We ran into the locker room. After putting on my uniform, I felt ready for anything. Chuck then directed me to the ring I was supposed to be in. There were about twenty kids, all bigger than me hanging around the ring, but they all looked nervous. Then I remembered something Sensei Lee had said in class. It was one of those tournament tricks,

"Keep your head up and look them in their eyes, you can intimidate them that way." So that's what I did, and you know what? It did work for some of them. Just then, the referees showed up, and they yelled,

"Line up by twos, shortest in the front."

And there I was right in the front, so you know what that meant. I was in the first match, but I wasn't nervous. I just wanted to get it over with. I thought to myself, *ok Sensei Lee, this is for you.*

The head referee called us up to face off in a space marked in tape in the shape of a big square. It was about ten feet by ten feet. They called it the ring. In the middle of the ring was an x. And that's where the head referee stood and waited for me and my opponent.

When we got there, I looked across at the boy I was about to spar, and he looked scared, which made me feel stronger. Then I remembered what sensei Lee taught us in the dojo,

"Let your punch guide your kick." I was ready to go, but the referee yelled,

"Hajime" which is pronounced "hah, jah may!" and means start in Japanese. My arm and fist zinged out straight towards the boy's chest and landed with a loud thump. Wapp! He then grabbed his chest and began to moan. The referee stopped us and awarded me a point. I was amazed that sparring was so easy.

We lined up again. The boy was terrified now, and I wasn't. The referee started us again, and as soon as I heard the command to start coming out of his mouth, my leg lifted, and my foot plunged into the boy's stomach. The impact hit him with such force that it bent him over, and he dropped to the floor. My confidence was growing then, and I realized that this is what it was all about. After that, the third and final point was easy, and there was my first win. After the match was over, I saw Chuck smiling and clapping. He said,

"All right, that was great, be careful of the next guy, I saw him fight before." I thought to myself, *next guy, there's a next guy*? I didn't know I had to fight again. But I did three more times, and they all turned out the same way; I was really kicking some serious butt, and when my fourth match was over, Chuck was there again, he yelled!

"Jeff, you win one more, you'll get first place, and you'll win a trophy!"

I thought to myself, *this is going to be easy. Put that trophy in the bag. I'm ready.* The head referee called us up and announced this was the final match for first place, and there I was, standing in front of the biggest ten-year-old I had ever seen before. He had bushy hair and bloodshot eyes, and his uniform was tight on him. I guess they couldn't find one big enough for him. He was a whole two heads taller than me.

I don't know if it was the noise of the crowd cheering or the size of the giant contestant I was about to fight, but for the first time at the tournament, I started getting nervous. I tried looking him in the eye, but it's hard to do that when you're looking up into his chest. I tried growling, but he growled right back, and his growl was louder. That's when I realized tricks wouldn't help me win this fight. I got to do what I got to do.

The referee was poised, ready to start the match. The giant stood there, also prepared. I think I was the only one concerned. When the referee gave the command to start, I froze, and I learned that if you let a big guy hit you, he will hurt you.

He punched me in the stomach so hard I think my mom and dad felt the pain at home. I bent over, looking at my feet, coughing, and even though I was in pain, I knew I had to suck it up. That was because Chuck yelled,

"Suck it up!" from the sideline.

This is what I was afraid of, getting my butt kicked in front of everybody, and there was nothing I could do about it. Then the referee called us up again. Well, here we go again. I looked up, and there he was. I was hoping he would disappear for some reason, but he didn't.

He stood there smiling, boasting to all his friends around the ring, and then the referee lined us up again. I was waiting for the command to start again. I wasn't going to let him hit me again, so I was prepared to block anything he threw at me. The ref yelled,

"START!" another quick punch came at me from his massive arms, which landed hard on my arm. Whew, the arm is not a point area. Even though it hurt, I was glad that I had stopped one of his strong advances, and then I got another surprise when all the referees yelled,

" Point!" I yelled back,

"What point? He punched me on my arm!" the head referee said,

"No back talk, get on the line and get ready to fight."

I didn't understand how he got a point. He hit me on my arm. What a rip off. Sensei Lee told me to expect many things, such as looking out for punches and kicks, but he never told me to look out for the referees. That upset me.

My mother and father always said something that I remembered, "Only dogs get mad." At that point, I became a dog because I got mad, and the fear left my body.

It was funny how I wasn't nervous anymore. I couldn't wait for the referee to line us up. I didn't care how big my opponent was. I didn't care if he was ahead of me in points. I was not going to go down without a fight. The referee lined us up again. It seemed like time was standing still. Everything was silent.

It was like I could see every muscle in my large opponent's arm finch, so when I heard the command to start, I saw his massive body coming towards me. I just slid my body to the right, picked up my left leg and lunged my foot into a wall of blubber, the impact knocked me to the floor, all I heard was a loud thud, the crowd cheering, and the referees yelling,

"POINT!" Man, did I get hit again, is it all over, but I didn't feel anything, but I then looked up, the referees were pointing at me, I got the point! Yes, here we go! I am ready, big boy doesn't look so big now, and that confident look he had on his face is gone. Chuck then yelled to me,

"It's time to win this match, hurry."

I wasn't sure what Chuck meant by that, but I was about to find out, the head referee lined us up again, and gave us the command to start, I leaped right at big boy with the swiftest punch I could throw, and was about a foot away from his fat belly, when I heard someone yell,

"TIME!" then felt two big hands grabbing me from behind, stopping my technique inches from his large, unprotected stomach, the referee then told us to stand and look at each other, then the referee pointed at big boy and said,

"TWO!" and then he pointed at me and said,

"ONE!" then he pointed at big boy again and said,

"WINNER!" the crowd cheered and booed, he then told us to bow to each other and shake hands, so I did, and after that it seemed like everybody in the gym came up to me and started shaking my hand. All I heard was,

"Good match, you'll get em next time." Heck, even big boys' mom, and dad came up to me and said,

" You took my boys heart, that will teach him." They even started calling me a nick name,

"Way to go speedy!" I walked over to Chuck and said,

"I'm sorry man, I lost, I don't know what happened?" Chuck then explained,

"Time ran out, that's all, and it's a good thing for large Louie, because you were taking that match over," just then Sensei Lee walk up to the ring and asked,

"How are we doing here?" A wave of sadness came over me and I responded,

"I'm sorry I let you down Sensei, I tried but I lost," Chuck hugged me from the side and yelled happily to sensei,

"He took second place!" Sensei Lee said, "Good more gold for us."

Just then I heard my name called. I looked up, and the referees were calling me to come back to the ring. Sad and frightened I walked back to the ring. When I got there I saw big boy and the other guy I had beaten. The head referee guided me to stand in the middle of them. From the corner of my eye I saw it, a trophy. It was shiny and gold, it stood about six feet tall and at the top there was a little karate man kicking.

I never saw a trophy as big as that before, and they were bringing it right to me... WOW!

And as soon as I thought they were going to hand it to me, they passed me and handed the fantastic award to the big boy, my heart dropped, but not for long, because I saw another trophy, it wasn't as tall, but it was shiny and gold, and it also had a karate man on top of it. This one they handed to me. In all my ten years on earth I never won anything but maybe a few basketball games over Greg and some other guys in my neighborhood, but I never got a trophy for it. I was so excited I felt I was going to faint. The moment the golden prize touched my hand, electricity filled my body. The thought of it only being second place didn't even enter my mind. I was on top of the world.

All the way back from the tournament I couldn't keep my eyes off my trophy. I couldn't wait for my mother and father to see it, and I knew my brother and sister was going to flip out, when they saw the trophy.

It was late when I got home, and nobody was awake. When I walked in the door it was dark. I wanted to wake everybody up and tell them what I had done but I wasn't sure how they would react. Even though I was really excited, I went to bed.

As I lay in my bed I pictured in my mind what I did, and I thought about all the things I should have done. All my training in class proved to be extremely helpful, it was like Sensei Lee said,

"The way is in training." I knew I wasn't going to be scared anymore. I was going to be ready next time.

Through all my contemplation that night, I realized why I lost. It wasn't because my opponent was better than me, it was because I had a small lack of confidence in my training. That is why Sensei Lee was so good. He trained hard and believed in himself. Now I know that's what I have to do, train hard so I will have no doubt in myself. I tossed and turned for hours till I finally drifted off to sleep.

The next morning I was awoken by a loud scream, I jumped up wondering who was screaming, I heard,

"YESS!" the voice sounded familiar, It was my mother, she must have discovered my trophy, after my usual morning yawn, scratch, and stretch, I walked downstairs and my mother was standing in the living room looking at my trophy just smiling, saying,

"That's my baby!" As I walked into the living room I was greeted with a big hug and kiss by my mother,

"You did it baby!" she yelled holding me tight, then out of the same breath she said,

"Did they hurt you?" I rolled my eyes and responded,

"No mom," and she kissed me again.

It really felt good that my mother gave me so much attention, my brother woke up from all the commotion and came down the steps to see what was going on. My mother showed him my great accomplishment and he was impressed. He picked up the trophy and said,

"This is really cool it even has a Karate guy on it. I think you should know that even though you won this trophy you still can't kick my butt." He smiled at me and put the trophy down.

At the dojo, the teachers acted like it was no big deal to them. Their philosophy was, no matter what you do, if you do your best, you will be rewarded, physically, mentally, or spiritually.

Training and winning at that tournament was great. It made me want more. So for months every time a tournament came up I asked to compete. And I did. And I won. I got second place sometimes, third every once in a while, but most of the time I got First!

Being a kid the one thing I didn't realize was that tournaments cost money. Before I came to that conclusion, all I knew was tell my dad and mom there was a tournament, they gave me money, and off to the tournament I would go.

Till one day a special tournament came up in Washington DC, I remember sitting in our Thursday class, Sensei Lee was ending class, with a big smile on his face he said,

"Students this is a great honor for our school. We have been invited to compete in the Washington DC Open Tournament. And one of the guests that will be there, is the Great Bruce Lee." The whole class jumped up and yelled,

"I WANT TO GO!"

Then Sensei Lee passed out the application's and said

"See you Saturday."

I was so excited. I was going to meet the great Bruce Lee. I ran all the way home.

I couldn't wait to tell my Mom and Dad. When I got home, my Mom was in the kitchen, and my Dad was in the living room watching TV. So of course I ran to my Mom handing her the application and said,

"There's a Tournament in Washington DC, and I'm going to kick some real butt because," but before I could get another word out, she said in a calm voice,

"I'm sorry honey you can't go."

For some reason what she said didn't reach my conscience mind. I was thinking I was already at the tournament. So the next words that came out of my mouth, I don't really remember because of my mother's reaction. I think I said,

"What the HELL are you talking about, I'm going and that is that!" Even though I had months of karate training, I learned at that moment that no matter how much training you have you never talked back to your Mom. I really couldn't say she hit me, because to be truthful I really didn't see anything, all I remember is getting up off of the floor. I do remember my Dad coming into the kitchen from the living room with his belt in his hand, ready to get his turn.

My mom stopped him and said with a calm voice again,

"I got this honey, go back at looking at TV."

With me now ready to listen, My mom explained to me what was going on. She told me that the tournaments that I was going to cost money. They love letting me go and show off my God given talent so much that they were both working odd jobs to pay for the tournaments. This week we had a problem, the water heater in our house went out. Every penny they earned went to that, so there was no tournament.

I went to bed feeling like we must be really poor. Dumb water heater, had to go out when Bruce Lee is coming. And I can't show off my God given talent to him. I know that was prideful, but I was just a kid.

It was funny the next day made me really realize there is a God. My Uncle Marvin came to our house, we haven't seen him since my birthday when he gave me my professional Spalding basketball.

I was in bed when I heard my mom scream out,

"Marvin!" That surprised me, I immediately ran down the steps to greet him. There he was loud and amusing, he could always make me laugh. It was ironic the first words out of his mouth,

"Haaeya, How's it going Bruce Lee!" I couldn't hold in my disappointment my head went down, I answered,

"Fine," I turned around and went back upstairs to my bed.

Well my Uncle Marvin stayed for a while and talked to my mom and dad. Before he took off, he yelled up the steps to me,

"KEEP KICKIN BUTT! But when he says butt, it starts an A.

About an hour later my mom and my dad called me,

"Jeff come down we want to talk to you." I reluctantly went down. My mom said firmly,

"You know, you were rude to your Uncle Marvin." I replied back apologetically,

"I know mom I'm sorry, my dad answered back,

"You knowing makes it worse." So then I explained my rude behavior.

"Dad, I'm sorry, I love Uncle Marvin, but when he mentioned Bruce Lee it got the best of me, because he is going to be at the tournament."

My mom and dad both yelled,

"Bruce Lee! You didn't tell us that!" Now I think I should have told them that first. They continued talking,

"We told your Uncle Marvin that you were rude because you couldn't go to the tournament but now we understand why you were so upset. The good news is despite your being rude to him he gave us the money so you can compete.

I believe I was blessed by God. I went to the tournament, I got first place sparring, and I even met the one and only Bruce Lee.

Three days later my Uncle Marvin died of a massive heart attack. Uncle Marvin was very special to me. It wasn't about the presents he gave me that made me love him so much. It was how he inspired and supported me.

Thanks Unc, I did KICK BUTT!

Can Students Learn How To Learn?

Days became weeks, weeks became months, months became years.

I was a little confused with my emotions, Since being in karate I was taught a lot of things about life. Many of my moms and dads' ways contradicted what I was taught in karate class. My mother always said,

"Honey don't fight."

Sensei Lee said,

"Fight when the opportunity presents itself."

My dad said,

"Stop yelling, don't make a lot of noise," Sensei Walt says,

"Use your voice as a weapon, (kia) or yell as loud as you can to scare your opponent."

For years, my parents tried to give me good parental wisdom, but my mom and dad didn't have a lot of education, so they did things that sometimes did not make a lot of sense to me. That was until I started taking karate. The karate way of thinking is one of discipline. Some people would call it cruel, but they did take pride in raising me in their own special way, how could I make this philosophy understandable. I like to call it the mother bird syndrome. The mother bird takes care of the baby birds for weeks, till one day the mother bird decides that the baby birds have stayed in the nest long enough. Then she begins to push the baby birds out of the nest one by one, and the baby birds either fly away up high in the sky or fall to the ground to an almost certain death. This seems a bit harsh, but it must work, or you would see hundreds of dead birds on the street, but you do see a lot of them flying in the sky.

Winter came in hard, snow, ice, freezing rain, kept me inside. All I did was train. Karate became my only way of thinking.

Now being fourteen my body was getting strong my feet and my hands became very rough. Because of my dedication, I could see the improvements in myself. But my teachers would never tell me. All the karate instructors would ever do was demand me to be perfect. They were always pushing me to do more. All I heard was punch harder, kick higher, and go longer. Sometimes I thought they were trying to get me to quit. But what I didn't know at the time was there was a method to their madness.

One day after a killer class, Sensei Lee and Sensei Walt was standing around with the other teachers, and he called me over,

"Jeff San, come here please," I ran over as fast as I could, and answered,

"Yes Sensei."

Sensei Walt jumped in my face and said harshly,

"Who are you yelling at boy?" I was shocked with his question, and replied,

"Sorry Sensei, I did not mean to yell at you." There I was standing in front of the top martial artist in the city, maybe the country, heck for all I knew, maybe the world, and they he had a problem with me, so I got a little concerned. Really I was ready to piss my pants, but I remembered something that Sensei Lee said,

"Never be afraid of me or any of your teachers. We are here to teach you." That was a great encouragement for me. He never failed to surprise me with his lessons. One time we were having a normal class, and I was taught two lessons at the same time, one of skill and good wisdom.

A new kid started in class, he was with us for about a week, his name was Tommy, he was sixteen years old, long stringy hair, six feet tall, and a little over weight, most of it was mouth. He was really cocky, and for some reason his face always looked dirty to me. He thought he knew everything and was always saying something stupid and getting punished for it. Even though he annoyed Sensei Lee, he trained Tommy with patience and calm composure.

Sensei Lee was showing us a new technique, he said,

"Today we are going to work on our mobility, moving from side to side could prevent you from getting hit," he then explained,

"If your attacker has a weapon you might not have to put your arms and hands in harm's way." That made perfect sense to me, but for some reason Tommy had a problem with that concept, and blurted out,

"I thought that's what karate was all about, making your arms and hands tough enough to Break baseball bats and stuff."

Sensei Lee acted like he didn't even hear him, he kept on teaching, but Sensei Walt was not having any of that, and he walked up to Tommy and said,

"Give me fifty pushups big mouth," Sensei Lee walked over and stopped Sensei Walt and said,

"No, he's right" the whole class was very shocked, we never saw a teacher challenge another teacher's decision. Sensei Lee had something up his sleeve, he walked over to Tommy, and then addressed the class,

"Class, young Tommy here wants to learn how to make his hands and arms tougher against weapons, this is a black belt lesson but today I'm going to make an exception." He then looked at Sensei Walt winked his eye and said,

"Get me the blade."

Sensei Walt left the dojo for a minute and came back with the biggest shiniest sword I had ever seen in my whole life. The whole class had their eyes fixed on the dangerous weapon. Sensei Lee then instructed Sensei Walt to stand across from him with the large sword, and then Sensei Lee said,

"I want you to break the sword with your arm." Then the two teachers bowed towards each other and squared off in an attacking stance. The class was shocked to see such a display. Sensei Walt and Sensei Lee both yelled, and their bodies started towards each other. Sensei Walt then suddenly thrusted the dangerous weapon at Sensei Lee's poised waiting arm. The whole class was eager to see the end of this exhibition. Then within an inch of contact, Sensei Lee yelled,

"Yame!" which means stop in Japanese. In a questioning voice Sensei Lee turned his attention to the class and said,

"Were you thinking that my arm was strong enough to block the sword?"

Before we could respond he continued,

"Sensei Walt is my arm tough enough?" Sensei Walt replied sarcastically,

"Yeah your arm is."

Sensei Lee continued his conversation with the class,

"Let's get back to reality. Moving your body out of the way of something is better than trying to block it with your arms and injuring yourself."

Sensei Lee looked around the class, and he fixed his eyes on Tommy, and said,

"Are your arms tough enough to block the sword?" Tommy now embarrassed by the sudden attention, answered nervously,

"No Sensei Lee." He responded,

"Perfect, then you will be the best student to become skilled at this technique, moving your body out of the way of harm."

Tommy was confused and answered,

"What do you mean Sensei?"

Sensei Lee put his hand on Tommy's shoulder, and said,

"The reality is that you cannot block everything. Sometimes you have to move your body out of the way."

Tommy wasn't the only one that learned a lesson from this threatening experience. I also learned that all teachers need admiration for putting up with naive students. Karate teachers especially because the martial arts is filled with unlimited concepts. Teaching martial arts to people that have a short attention span is difficult.

With Rank Comes Responsibility

When I reached the rank of green belt watching and training under Sensei Lee and Sensei Walt it made me want to become a black belt. It also inspired me to want to teach their extraordinary art to others.

When I got the chance I told Sensei Lee of my desires. One day after a great class, all of the other students had left, and Sensei Lee was dressed and ready to go home, that's when I approached him, with respect and said,

"Sensei may I talk to you sir?" I was so nervous. I didn't know why. Sensei Lee was always open to hearing what his students had to say. He answered me with a concerning voice,

" What's up buddy?" I must admit it did calm me, I replied nervously,

"Sensei Lee I really want to be a black belt," he answered sternly,

"Why?" His reply surprised me a little. I answered,

"I don't know?"

Sensei Lee said smugly, "If you don't know why, then you will never be a black belt of mine, just forget it kid." He turned and started to walk away. I was very insulted, so I replied loudly,

"Forget it! I can't forget it! Sensei your teaching changed my life! All I think about is martial arts now! All the pain of training, the cuts, the bruises. Sensei I don't know how to do anything else, why are you telling me to forget it?" With his back to me, he answered,

"With rank comes responsibility, boy, are you ready for that?" I answered confidently,

"I was born ready sensei, just give me a chance," Sensei Lee turned around smiling, then he said something that kind of scared me, he looked straight at me with a crazy look in his eyes and said,

"You may have been ready when you were born, but we'll see if you're ready now."

Without another word, he turned and walked away. Why did I tell sensei that I wanted to be a black belt? Because soon after that, karate classes changed, training became more intense.

Sensei Lee started treating me differently. He showed me all the Japanese katas. Katas were punches and kicks in the air as if you were fighting someone. They were used to help you keep your balance and strengthen your body. Learning these different fighting techniques also helped my memory. There were fifty kata's all together. He only taught me ten of them to start. Sensei Lee said,

"You will learn the rest of them, when it is time to learn them." I wasn't sure what he meant by that. I wasn't worried about that either, I just liked doing the ones he taught me.

Two weeks after I told him my karate choice. I walked into karate class as usual. I wasn't expecting anything different but what happened changed my life forever. There were about fifteen students in class that day, all of us were ready to learn. Sensei Lee walked up to the front of class as he always did and yelled,

"Hajamay! "The command to start class. We all lined up, then Sensei Lee said,

"We all need to understand that we should be careful of what we wish for, because we just might get it." He looked straight at me and said,

"Jeff come up to the front and warm up the class." Everybody was shocked, including myself. Immediately I noticed Sensei Walt approach Sensei Lee and the two men stood face to face and they began talking in whispers to each other. I imagined Sensei Lee was explaining to Sensei Walt why he asked me to lead the class.

I stood up there and stared at the class. The students were no help they just stood there waiting for me to lead them. I was so nervous, I wanted to pee myself. I thought to myself, *what am I doing? I'm no teacher.* I was ready to run out of the classroom. Then something came to me. This is what I've been waiting for. I've seen all the teachers in class do it a million times. The little voice inside my head said,

This is your chance man. Sensei told you to start the class.

It took all the courage in my body, but I was finally able to start teaching the class. At that moment I remembered something that Sensei Lee said,

"He who seeks his path, will find his path." So I put all my fears aside and brought a loud voice from the bottom of my diaphragm,

"SINGLE PUNCHES, RIDING HORSE STANCE POSITION!"

The whole class was shocked, they seemed surprised that I could yell that loud. I actually was surprised myself. I thought if I didn't do it right I might not get another chance. I gave it my best shot and I felt the class was going great. The students all moved with great precision. I thought they were moving so well because of me, but the real reason was because of Sensei Lees teaching. They were taught to give respect to whoever is running the class. I didn't care I was having a ball, and it made me think about something else sensei said,

"Doing what you like is freedom, liking what you do is happiness."

The class ran with no problems. Sensei Lee appeared to be impressed as he observed and nodded, but I noticed that Sensei Walt held a stern emotionless stance. After class was over, as me and the other students were heading towards the door to leave, I noticed the two teachers walking into the office. I became curious about what they might be discussing and decided to go back close to the door and listen. I heard Sensei Walt say skeptically,

"Do you think Jeff has what it takes to be a black belt?" Sensei Lee replied,

"I have to admit, he's good. His skills and techniques have improved, and he really has shown that he is determined." Sensei Walt responded,

"Kids his age usually do well, and then they get bored, and quit." Sensei Lee replied,

"I don't think so, this kid looks like he is serious. Don't worry man he'll be my special project." I smiled and turned to leave. I was right, I had impressed at least Sensei Lee and from my perspective he was the most important. I would soon learn that the two teachers were going to start training me differently.

A few weeks later, the whole class was working out our arms.

That meant we were going to do punches, blocks, pushups, and plenty of them. Well it felt like we did about five thousand of each, and we were starting to get a little sloppy, and all of a sudden, Sensei Lee gave us the command to stop,

"Yahmay!" We really only did about fifty sets of each, but that didn't mean anything. We were expected to do our best all the time. Then I got a shocking surprise, Sensei Walt glared at me, and then he called me sternly,

"Jeff, up to the front of class!" At first I thought I was called to work the class out again.

I ran up with lofty expectations, but boy was I wrong, I responded,

"Yes Sensei," Sensei Lee yelled,

"Boy is that the way you're supposed to do your techniques in this class!" I answered,

"No Sensei." I must admit I did look a little sloppy, but heck everybody was looking sloppy, Sensei Lee fussed at me some more,

"Do you have a problem with this work out?" I answered nervously,

"No, not really Sensei." He yelled again,

"Not really, I don't understand that, explain that to me!" I was really scared now, I didn't know what to say, and I answered,

"Well we did a lot of blocks, and I think my arms got a little tired." When the word tired came out my mouth, I thought Sensei Lee was going to have a fit, he screamed,

"Tired. You're tired?" Because of his state the class knew there was a problem. Sensei Lee turned and looked at the rest of class and yelled,

" Is anybody else tired!" the whole class answered,

"No Sensei!" Wow, they didn't back me up at all. I felt like I was on a deserted island, and I didn't think there were any rescue plans. Sensei Lee seemed to calm down, he said,

"Alright, since Jeff is the only one who's tired, we should give him a break."

I heard what he said but for some reason, I didn't really think I was going to get a break, and I was right.

Sensei Lee told me to sit in a chair, and then he left the dojo. Maybe I was going to get a break, but that fantasy bubble busted.

Sensei Lee returned with two red house bricks, he handed the two bricks to me, and placed one in each hand, and he pulled my arms out straight in front of me, then he said,

"Every time the bricks go down, the class does twenty pushups."

Sensei Lee turned and resumed teaching the class. At first I thought *these bricks didn't feel that heavy,* but after about a minute I started feeling a little different. Sensei Lee started taunting me,

"Your arms getting tired boy?"

Then he continued teaching, three minutes went by, my arms started feeling strange, but I wasn't going to let those bricks down. I did start watching the clock though. I thought to myself, *just an hour and thirty minutes to go,* Sensei Lee, started taunting again,

"Don't you want to let the bricks down, and give your weak classmates their pushups?"

His taunting would have probably bothered other guys, but it just made me more determined. All of my class mates were watching me carefully. I am sure there were wondering if I was going to let those bricks down.

Even though my arms were getting tired. I wanted to keep those bricks up, but not for them. I wanted to keep the bricks up for me. After a while, my whole body started feeling the pressure of the two bricks in my hands, but I refused to let those bricks down. Now I started getting mad. What did holding two bricks up have to do with karate? And why did Sensei make me responsible for the rest of the class?

I began to feel that Sensei Lee was not being fair to me or the rest of the class. We were only taking a little break, so what if we were not working hard. In the middle of that thought Sensei Lee walked over to me, and looked me in the eyes, and said,

"Is there a problem boy?" I answered,

"No sensei!" Sensei Lee screamed,

"I think you do have a problem, you would rather hold bricks, than practice the right way."

And that's when it hit me. Sensei Lees taunting helped me remember something that Sensei Walt said a long time ago,

"If you practice inferior, you will be inferior."

I also remembered the day I told Sensei Lee of my desire to be a black belt. He asked if I was ready for the additional responsibilities that came with that rank. It didn't dawn on me then but now it was clear that being able to teach was one of those responsibilities.

Most teachers of martial arts do their best to teach their students the techniques they need to learn the arts. However because the students get bored with training, they sometimes don't appreciate the full purpose of the lessons.

I told Sensei Lee I wanted to be a black belt, but because of my lack of interest at times it created some doubt or concern.

The only way I was going to prove to Sensei Lee that I wanted to be a black belt, was by being a better student. If he wanted me to hold bricks up as a punishment so be it. I held those bricks up until the end of class.

After class was over, I was sore, but I was also embarrassed for how I acted. So slowly I walked over to Sensei Lee, I bowed and said,

"I'm sorry sensei, I let you down," Sensei Lee answered,

"What are you talking about?"

I replied,

"In class today, I didn't give you the proper respect," Sensei Lee, said,

"What do you mean, you didn't give me respect?" I answered,

"By not trying hard," then Sensei Lee blew my mind with his explanation,

"Do you really think I had you hold those bricks because you didn't give me respect?" he chuckled and continued,

"No Jeff holding those bricks were not a punishment. It was an opportunity." Then I was puzzled, and I asked,

"An opportunity?" Sensei Lee explained,

"Yes, Jeff, this was an opportunity. You told me you wanted to be a black belt. One of the things you have to learn is that you must be thought of as superior by your classmates, physically, mentally, and spiritually. The only way to become stronger is by practicing. Holding those bricks made your arms a little stronger, and that was the physical part of it. By keeping the bricks up in front of your classmates, well you could say that was the mind part of it. You could have very easily dropped those bricks a few times. But you didn't and your classmates admire you for that," I answered abruptly,

"But sensei, the truth is, I didn't hold the bricks up for them, I held them up because I was afraid of you." He responded,

"That was the best part of your opportunity. The class doesn't have to know why you kept the bricks up. All they need to know is that you keep the bricks up. That made them admire you a bit, it might have made you look stronger to your class mates. This training method is a double edge sword for us.
My goal was to make you stronger, not only in body, but your mind as well. Your so-called punishment was a two-part experiment. One to make you stronger, and two for you to gain some respect with the other students." I answered skeptically,

"But sensei, what if I had dropped the bricks?" Sensei Lee smiled and said,

"Then we wouldn't be having this conversation, would we? I have plans, just like you have plans. You want to become a black belt which includes being able to teach, and I want to help you. But before you can teach, you must know how to learn. Jeff it is often said, *'a journey of a thousand miles must begin with a single step.'* At first you thought this lesson was a waste of time, didn't you?" I answered,

"Kind of," Sensei replied,

"Nothing is a waste of time if you learn from it. You did well today and if you trust me in the end, both of us will get what we want. Just go home, and get some rest, you're going to need it, we have a long way to go."

I turned and walked away. Even though he told me I did well, I didn't know what was in store for me.

The Way Is In Training

After that day, Sensei Walt started pushing me and working my body during every class. I think he wanted to make sure that Sensei Lee had made the right choice. It felt like he stepped up all practices just for me. Every class became an intense experience. I trained under the watchful eye of Sensei Walt.

Now, I didn't get any breaks. No excuses were allowed. It was all or nothing. Sensei Lee even had me run some classes which came with plenty of criticism from Sensei Walt. But I didn't let it disturb me. All I knew was that karate training was now becoming a challenge. It was one that I was willing to take. I was amazed at how many different ways my Sensei could motivate me. My strength improved because of more difficult karate techniques.

One day, as I made my way to the dojo, I spotted Sensei Lee standing on the street corner. I approached him with a bow, a gesture of respect and greeted him,

"Hello Sensei,"

"Hello Jeff, I was waiting for you." I was very flattered that Sensei was waiting for me. I couldn't wait to hear what Sensei had to say. We both started walking to the dojo together. Sensei began to explain why he was waiting for me,

"Jeff, you have won some big karate tournaments, and that's great, but now it's time for you to understand something about life, I answered, puzzled,

"About life?" Sensei said,

"Yeah life. Look around you Jeff. People walking here and there, going up or down. They all have different professions and do other things. Most of them all have the same stereotypical thinking about people who study

Karate. They believe that we are superhuman, that we can walk through walls, break bricks with our heads," I interrupted,

"But sensei, you do break bricks with your head," he replied,

"Exactly, we do a lot of amazing things, but why? Because we train hard, we push our bodies and minds to great limits. It takes many years of dedication and endless training. Just remember, you can be as good as you are, or you can be as good as people think you are. But if you are a real martial arts student, you will never be as good as you want to be. Remember perfection is what you strive for, until you reach that, you should never be satisfied."
I questioned Sensei,

"Sensei, how will I know when I have reached perfection?" Sensei Lee answered,

"You'll never know. But everybody around you will know."

We continued walking and Sensei Lee then started explaining his unique plan to me,

"Jeff, martial arts is my life. I have been training and teaching in the martial arts for fifty-five years. I have given up worldly pleasures, sacrificed jobs and relationships, I've put myself in mortal danger, all for the learning and teaching the martial arts." I curiously replied,

"You make karate sound like it's a religion." Sensei Lee quickly replied,

"You see that's the problem Jeff. Everyone thinks religion is so right and so serious, and everything else is just something else. To me there is not a difference between the two."
I questioned,

"Why is that Sensei?" Sensei Lee explained,

"I have helped my students, not only with karate but with life, but now I'm getting older. I realize I'm not going to live forever, but I do want what I teach to my students to go on long after I am gone. The only way that can happen is if someone can go on teaching it. Jeff you are the one I have chosen to do that. You remind me of me when I was young, your thirst for knowledge and perfection." I interrupted,

"Sensei, you are not that old," Sensei Lee smiled and then continued.

"For a rock or maybe a tree, I am not that old. But for a fly or a flower, I am ancient." He always said things like that to make me think. Sensei explained,

"I have to have time to teach you, it will take a while. You see Jeff, I never had any kids of my own. The only kids I had were the ones I teach in my classes because martial arts means so much to me." I nodded and he continued,

"I need to know that the school will go on being taught by someone that will teach it like me. Someone that is as serious about training and teaching as well as helping all the students."

It was comforting yet also a little scary hearing that Sensei Lee had chosen me. I wasn't sure if I could fulfill his big plan, but I knew I had to try. Then Sensei Lee continued,

"I have planned five distinct stages of your training. Today, you will be starting the first, it's called earth training. It helps test your body and mind." After he said that, we silently walked the rest of the way to the dojo. I was a little nervous but very ready to start training.

When we got to the center, sensei said,

"Go in and start class, I'll be there in a minute."

I walked into the dojo. To my amazement, I saw a large tree stump in the middle of the dojo.

I walked up to the huge obstacle and touched it. I couldn't believe it was in the dojo because the sensei always talked about keeping the dojo clean. And it wasn't too clean.

It was hard and rough around the outside and flat and smooth on the top. Just then, Sensei Lee walked in. He walked up to me and said,

"This is your new best friend," I was confused by that comment and said,

"What?" sensei replied,

"That's what, sir," Because of my confusion, I forgot my respect. I quickly replied,

"What sir?" I was very intrigued, and sensei Lee saw that I was eager to see what he had in mind to do with the large stump, so sensei then explained,

"Balance is another one of the things you need." He then instructed me to stand top of the stump. I jumped up on the stump and looked around. Being on the stump felt strange. My body was very shaky, moving back and forth. Sensei Lee walked up to me and said,

"Now you learn balance." Suddenly he started throwing punches at me and yelled,

"Block!" It felt like hundreds of punches were being hurled at me, and all I could do was move. Then I realized I was elevated off the stump. I was paying so much attention to sensei's massive attack. I took the wrong step and fell. I don't know why, but I felt stupid. I put my head down and said,

"Sorry, sensei," Sensei Lee said,

"Why are you sorry Jeff, that's why you practice, so you achieve balance, you will get it. Try again."

So I did, over and over, and I fell, over and over again. We continued with this lesson for weeks. One day while Sensei was pelting me with punches over and over again, then all of a sudden, I realized that I hadn't fallen.
I stood there on top of that stump with astonishment and said,

"Sensei I didn't fall." Then Sensei Lee said something I will never forget,

"So what? Do you want a cookie? It's about time, and I thought you would never get it. My arms were getting tired of knocking you off that stump." It took a long time for me to realize I had to block with my arms and not move my body. Sensei always said,

"Trust in your arms, it makes it easier for you to keep your balance." After months of training, to my bewilderment, not falling off that stump was a small accomplishment.

Then I understood why Sensei Lee constantly worked my body and mind. At the time, I thought I was really doing something great. In reality all I was doing was what was expected of me. If you want to find a good teacher, you have to find a good student, and and I didn't want to disappoint him ever again.

I trained on that stump for a few more weeks and started getting good at blocking on the stump.

One week later, I was at home, sleeping in my bed. I was having a good dream about me and the prettiest girl in my class. Then I heard my mom yell,

"Jeff, there is somebody hear to see you!" I looked at the clock. It was five o'clock in the morning. I wondered who would be there to see me. When I came down the steps I was surprised to see Sensei Lee. I looked at him with sleep in my eyes. He said in a bright, energetic voice,

"Let's go boy," I looked at my mom, she said,

"You said you wanted to take karate, so get going."

She was right, so I got dressed and went with Sensei Lee. I found it hard to predict what Sensei was going to do. I thought we were going to the dojo. Instead, I found myself at the bridge close to where I lived, and on each side of the bridge was a wall about a mile long. Sensei

Lee jumped up on the wall, turned to me, and said,

"Join me for a run." I was scared, but I jumped up with him and realized why I should have been scared. I looked down, and it was about a hundred feet down to a highway below. Sensei Lee then said,

"Let's run." I turned and started running on top of the wall across the bridge. Even though I was scared I was compelled to follow him. So I started running. As we ran further I grew tired and happened to glance down. I began to feel dizzy and momentarily lost my balance and stumbled. I thought I would fall when I suddenly felt Sensei Lee grab my hand and pull me straight, keeping me up on top of the wall. He yelled,

" You looked down, didn't you? "I took a breath," I answered, terrified,

"Yes, Sensei."

Sensei Lee then said something that helped me, not just then, but for the rest of my life,

"If you keep looking down, you will end up right where you are looking. You must pay attention to where you are, and what you are doing. Then you will get to where you are going with no problems. This is the second stage of your training, and it is called air."

Sensei Lee ensured I was alright, and then we started running again, but I didn't look down anymore. And my near-life-threatening experience gave me more concentration and assertiveness to make it the rest of the way across the wall of the bridge. It made me understand the difference between life and death.

This is why this stage is called air. When I lost my balance, all I thought about was I was going to die. When I first started karate, all I wanted to do was show some people that they could not take advantage of me. Then, after the first couple of years, I learned that martial arts was more than a sport or a fighting tool. It was starting to become a way of life for me.

About a month went by, I was over my last near-death experience, and I was concentrating in class. We had an average back-breaking class. We all enjoyed the sparring because Sensei Lee had us spar blindfolded. It helped us improve our reactions. It did make my reflexes improve, and I felt more aware. Sensei Lee announced that the class was going on a camping trip when the class ended. All of the students yelled,

"Alright!" I heard about camping, but I had never gone camping before. I didn't know what the big fuss was about. All I knew was I better get ready.

The day of the camping trip we were all excited and since I had never been camping before, I wasn't sure what to pack. When we got into the van to head to the camp site. All the other kids kept saying how excited they were for the night time. I had no idea what was so special about the nighttime.

When we arrived at the campsite we were told to go get wood. A few other guys and I set out to go get wood. Little did we know that since it had rained the night before all of the wood was damp and slimy. We gathered what felt like a ton of wood and piled it all in one spot. Sensei Walt came up and saw the massive pile of wood and said,

"That's nowhere near enough, go out and gather more." All of us set out to find more wood. We were digging up wood from the ground that had fallen, knocking down branches and anything we could to add to the wood pile. When we returned and Sensei Walt was satisfied he said,

"Okay now everyone can go set up your sleeping areas." That's when I realized that I was not prepared since I did not own or bring a tent. I thought we would be sleeping indoors in cabins. There I was standing looking like a fool without any equipment. Luckily for me my good friend Eddie who noticed me standing there looking lost and somewhat defeated said,

"Hey Jeff, come with me. You can help me set up my tent and you can bunk with me tonight."

After Eddie and I had set up our tent we both turned back towards the site where we had placed the wood and noticed that Sensei Walt and a few of the older kids had piled about half of the wood up. The logs were piled up about 4 feet around and 2 feet high. Sensei Walt yelled,

"Start the fire!"

One of the older students walked around the perimeter of the logs with a little metal can sprinkling liquid onto the wood. Once he walked around the entire circle another student threw a match on the logs and the next thing we heard was a loud "poof" and the bonfire was lit.

Sensei Walt admired the fire for a few minutes and then he went to the van. When he returned he had several bags which he handed to the older students. One by one they emptied the bags and to our surprise and delight there were hotdogs, beans, and chips.

We all sat around the bonfire as the food cooked and when we were finished eating Sensei Walt told us all to go change into our karate uniforms. Within 10 minutes we were all dressed in our uniforms and following Sensei Lee. After about five minutes we came upon a beautiful lake. After just a few brief minutes of us admiring the beauty of our surroundings Sensei Walt said,

"Okay all of you get in the water." Most everyone was extremely excited except for me since I did not know how to swim. I said,

"Uh Sensei Walt, I can't swim." He smirked and said,

"That's okay Jeff the water is only about chest high."

I relaxed a bit and slowly got in.   I noticed that everyone else was in and just as he said it was only up to most everyone's chest. The water was chilly and cloudy. Sensei Walt said,

"This is the stage of water. Okay pair off and start fighting each other." There were 12 of us so everyone had a partner. I thought how Sensei Walt had every detail planned, having the exact number of students.

Executing the karate techniques in the water was much more difficult than I anticipated. It took me a few minutes to get the hang of throwing kicks and punches but eventually I got it. My only concern was I was paired up with Eddie and I didn't want to whoop him too bad since he offered to allow me to share his tent with him for the night.

We stayed in the water for about an hour. Sensei Walt stopped us and said,

"Everyone did pretty well. Did you all have fun?" In unison we all responded,

"Yes Sensei."

We dragged ourselves out of the lake and with our soaked clothes we walked back to our campsite.

After changing into dry clothes we ate again. I was amazed at how dark it was. I had never seen anything like it before. The only thing we could see was the fire burning and glimpses of each other across the bonfire. Sensei Walt stood and said,

"The next stage is fire. Now I want you to all line up and run and jump over the bonfire." Some of the students stepped back while shaking their heads, no. I was intrigued so I stepped forward. Sensei Walt nodded to acknowledge me. I then took several steps back then ran full speed ahead towards the bonfire and jumped and performed a perfect side kick over the flames. I barely made it to safety on the other side of the bonfire. When I landed I heard collective sighs of relief and disbelief from my classmates. I turned back and waited for the next person to try it. Everyone cheered me on and gave me high fives but nobody else tried it. Next Sensei Walt said,

"Now it's time for run rabbit." Run Rabbit was a game similar to hide and go seek. One person ran into the woods to hide and everyone else would pursue that person and when they caught up to them and fought that person. In essence it was eleven against one. Each person took a turn being the rabbit, the person being pursued. Everyone had taken their turn as the rabbit including Eddie who was the last person before it was supposed to be my turn. After seeing Eddie being beaten until his pants came off. I decided I did not want to play this game, and I decided to find a place to hide. I heard frequent yells and playful banter in the distance until I drifted off to sleep.

When I awoke in the morning, I made my way back to the campsite by the bonfire. All I saw was smoke and people sleeping everywhere. It seemed that no one actually slept in their tents. Sensei Walt woke up and told us all to gather our things to prepare to leave but first we had to jog around the woods. While we jogged Sensei Walt pointed out things in the woods that he felt were important for us city kids to see and know about. Things such as moss on the side of a tree, several types of birds and even poison ivy.

Eventually he took us down a dirt path which led us back to the campsite and we packed our things into the van and headed back to the city. For a city kid it was a very enjoyable trip.

Student Becomes the Teacher

Weeks later, I went to class. When I got there, Sensei Walt was standing at the door. He said,

"Hey Jeff, Sensei Lee and I have to go somewhere, we need you to teach class today." I answered nervously,

"By myself?" Sensei Walt answered, scolding,

"Yes by yourself, you got a problem with that?" I taught the class many times but never without Sensei Lee or Walt in the building. I answered bravely,

"No Sensei," even though I was a little concerned, I knew I could do it.

That day in class, I was lucky. I only had five younger students, so I knew I could handle it. Class started fine, but as I trained them to punch, I realized Larry needed to work harder on his punching techniques. He was playing around. So I went over to him and said calmly,

"Punch harder," but he was not in the mood to hear what I had to say.

I never could understand why kids would come to class and play around. They were always getting in trouble with Sensei Lee or Sensei Walt. Now that they weren't there all of the discipline was up to me. I thought about what Sensei Lee would do if he were there. Larry didn't think he had to listen to me. He even ignored me. He continued to ignore my commands, so I spoke to him again, a little louder,

"Larry, I said Punch harder!" Then Larry whined,

"I don't feel like it." That's when I started thinking about all the training I had from Sensei

Lee and Sensei Walt. That's when I remembered something Sensei Lee said,

"First they ignore you, then they attack you, then you win."

I knew I had to do something fast because if I didn't, the other students would stop listening too, so I yelled,

"Larry, I didn't ask you how you felt. I said punch harder!" Larry was very disrespectful. He turned to me and said,

"You're not sensei, I don't have to listen to you." All I heard was the other students starting to laugh,

"ha ha ha." So I did what I thought Sensei Lee would do. I kicked Larry in the stomach and punched him in his chest, then I grabbed him and threw him to the floor. Because of my experience, I knew Larry couldn't beat me, so I wasn't worried about his retaliation. That's when I brought the class back in order. I announced,

"You see, class, that's why you have to train hard." I turned and looked down at Larry and said calmly,

"Get up, get in line, and punch harder." Larry jumped up, got in line, and started punching harder. After that, the class ran smoother.

The next day, I told Sensei Lee what I did because I was a little worried about Larry. I told Sensei Lee I thought Larry would be mad at me. Sensei Lee said,

"You're worried about if Larry is mad at you, hell, you should be mad at him. Jeff I gave you a job, to train my students, Larry disrespected you that means, he disrespected me. You did what you were supposed to do." I responded,

"But sensei, what if he's mad and he might not like karate anymore?" Sensei smiled and said,

"Jeff he's not mad at you, he fears you." I questioned,

"Sensei, do I want him to fear me?" Sensei Lee then explained his theory,

"If a student fears you or likes you, it doesn't matter, what a student has to do is respect you. I found that most students listen to me when they fear me, and they take advantage if they like me." I then said,

"Sensei, I like you," Sensei Lee looked me in the eye and said,

"That's because you have respect Jeff, that's the main reason why I am training you to be a teacher of my art. Don't worry about Larry, Jeff, he'll get over it, and his fear will turn into respect towards you". Sensei Lee always had a way of saying precisely what I needed to hear.

The End Becomes The Beginning

Through the years, classes changed. There were more katas, and they were more intense. We participated in more tournaments. I was seventeen now and more was expected of me by everyone. I never really thought about what Sensei Lee would teach me next. It just happened, and one day I realized I had been in martial arts for almost half my life. Many students came and left, and the longer I trained with Sensei Lee, the more I learned about karate and life. He also started giving me increased responsibility. I knew I was ready because of all I had learned.

One day, I was walking to karate class when I saw this fine girl. Not just a girl, but a woman. Long firm sexy legs, tight round butt, thin waist, flat belly, big full beautiful breasts, big black afro, and her face wasn't bad either.

But the best part was that she looked at me with a look on her face like she was in a five-star restaurant, and I was the best thing on the menu. That look gave me the confidence to go over and talk to her. When I opened my mouth to speak to her. I gave her my best line,

"Excuse me miss, you could make my life complete if you would tell me your name?" She smiled and said,

"Then let me complete your life. My name is Ronda. How are you doing, Jeff Washington?" I was shocked she knew my name. So I replied, amazed,

"You know my name?" She responded with a sweet, sexy voice,

"I know a lot about you Mr. Washington."

I was so excited. No one had ever called me Mr. Washington before. Then I began to wonder, what did she know about me? For some reason, I wanted this flirting to go on, so I had to come up with a quick line. I smiled, tilted my head low, looked into her eyes, and said,

"A lot is not all. Would you like to learn more?" That line must have worked because she turned and muttered seductively,

"Yes."

Then, all of a sudden, I remembered where I was going. I wanted to stay and talk with Ronda, but I knew I would be late for class if I waited any longer. Ronda then noticed the strange look on my face and asked me,

"Is there something wrong?" I thought to myself. What a woman. She could even tell when I had a problem. I wanted to talk to her about karate class, but I didn't know if she would understand my devotion to karate. I didn't even understand sometimes.

I felt like a deep-sea fisherman. I knew I had her hooked, and I didn't want her to get away. But if she knew so much about me, she had to know about my art, so I decided to just be honest with her and I said,

"I would love to stay here and talk to you a bit longer but I'm on my way to karate class right now and I do not want to be late." She smiled and said,

"I understand Mr. Washington. You go ahead to class and afterwards you can come to my place to visit."

Then she told me where she lived and mentioned that she lived alone. But the best part was that she would gladly wait to see me after class. After that, she winked and whispered in my ear,

"I'll be waiting."

I walked away from her, looking back at her the whole time. I couldn't keep my eyes off her until I was at least a block away.

I was so excited about my date after karate class that I couldn't focus on anything. Everybody noticed, especially Sensei Lee. Let's say I was off my game. When class was over, I hurried and got dressed, and I was heading towards the door when Sensei Lee called to me,

"Who's the girl?" I was embarrassed. I said,

"What, who, huh?" He continued,

"Only a girl could make you act like you did tonight." Sensei Lee wasn't just my teacher. He was also my friend, so I told him about Ronda. He leaned his head back and said,

"A wise man knows where he is all the time, an unwise man doesn't care." I thought to

myself, *there goes that fortune cookie thing again.* So
I had to ask,

"What does that mean?" Then he told me,

"Women destroy the best men. Always
remember, know where are, and who you are,
then realize what you are, and never be afraid." I
looked at Sensei Lee with a puzzled look on my
face and said,

"Thank you."

I was confused but didn't care because I
had a date with Ronda. I smiled all the way to
Ronda's house, and I didn't even know why. It
could be because I couldn't wait for the great
conversation we were going to have. Maybe
because I wanted her to be my girlfriend? Or
perhaps because I was a virgin, and I thought
Ronda was going to give me some? Yeah, it was
the virgin thing. I felt like such a dog, but I

couldn't help it. She threw me a bone, and I only wanted to give it back to her.

Arriving at her house, I was nervous. I almost turned around to go back home, but I was so intrigued about the possibilities. That and my hormones were raging and could have knocked on the door themselves, if you know what I mean. I was going nowhere but into that house.

I knocked on the door and waited about a minute, and then Ronda came to the door. She was wearing next to nothing, and I liked it that way. I don't know why but she seemed a little nervous. It didn't faze me one bit because it calmed me down a little. She said,

"Hi, Jeff, come in!" There was no sexy banter. She just hurried me in. Wow, this chick can't wait to get her hands on me. So we walked up her steps into her apartment. Her place looked great. It was small, and you had to walk through her kitchen to get to her living room, but it was nice and neat. I liked that you could see her bedroom from the front door. When we got in the house, Ronda seemed to calm down. Ronda said,

"Sit down, get comfortable. Would you like something to drink?" I wasn't thirsty, but I said,

"Sure."

She got me a glass of the coldest, sweetest iced tea I had ever tasted. After that, I was ready for whatever came next. She then sat down beside me, and we started with sexy talk. Much to my dismay the sexy talk didn't last long. Just when I thought it was about to get busy up in here. We heard a loud BANG at the front door. Followed by two more equally loud knocks like the police, BAM! BAM! Ronda jumped up and yelled,

"OH, NO!" So, of course, I said,

"What's the matter!" She then said,

"I think that's my ex-boyfriend." Because of my raging hormones and intense interest in her, I never asked her much about herself. Hell, I didn't even know her last name. But after she said boyfriend, I figured I would learn a lot about her real quick. Ronda said,

"I don't know what he wants. We broke up last night." I thought to myself, *Last night?*

Ronda instructed me to remain seated and said she would get rid of him. I didn't know why, but for some reason, I felt like this night wasn't going to turn out as I had expected.

Ronda left the room, and seconds later, a short, skinny black guy walked towards me. And the look on his face indicated to me that he was not happy. The other thing that told me that he was not pleased was his mean tone of voice when he barked,

"MAN you better GET OUT!" well, actually, that was enough to make me leave. But Ronda said in a scared voice,

"Jeff, I don't want you to leave."

Well, that's all I needed to hear for me to stay. It was out of the ordinary, but I figured that since he heard her say that she didn't want me to go, that meant he would have to go. Besides, if I leave, he might hurt her, and nobody's going to break my woman. Well, that's what I thought. So, I remained seated on the couch. I was so bold to say,

"Man, I'm not going anywhere."

I even crossed my arms and turned my back to him. Well, then, all of a sudden, I heard a BONG! It sounded like a Chinese gong. And for some reason, my head started to hurt, it got cloudy, and the room seemed to be spinning. I shook my head and looked around, and then I realized I was on my hands and knees on the living room floor.

Well, what had happened was, when I turned my back to him, that crazy guy took a metal chair from the kitchen and hit me over my head. That's when I realized he must really want me to leave. Well, I shook my head again, got myself together, and managed to get to my feet just in time.

Because in my lightheaded state, I thought the guy was going after Ronda. And that was lucky for me because, after his first attack, he could have quickly finished me off. His back was towards me. Now, it's my turn to give him a cheap shot. He was just about to hit Ronda. When I balled up my fist and punched him in the back of his head, I saw his head snap forward and back, and that stopped his aggression towards Ronda. Then I grabbed him and pulled him away from her, then he grabbed me, and we started wrestling around the room. I was swirling around so fast that I started getting sick; I wanted to throw up. But I didn't want him to see my weakness, so I held it in. He kept yelling,

"GET OUT! GET OUT!" So I started yelling,

"YOU GET OUT!"

I was trying to kick him, but we were too close, and because he was holding my arms, I couldn't give him a good punch either. All we did for the next five minutes was to wrestle around the apartment. Then he started to pull me towards the kitchen, and I slid and rammed right into the kitchen table. When I did, the force of the contact lifted his arm, giving me just enough room to knee him in his ribs, and that's what I did. That was the only thing that slowed him down. So I did it again. And I heard him shout.

"You mother!"

I wouldn't let him finish the rest of his statement because I put my hand over his mouth. That just made him madder, and he tried to bite me. Because of where my hands were, that gave him room to reach up and put his hands around my neck, and he tried to choke me. That's when I pulled one of his arms down, drawing me in close enough to stick my elbow in his face. And wouldn't you know it, he tried to bite me again. So I pushed my elbow deeper into his face.

We wrestled until we tussled out the apartment's front door and spilled into the second-floor hall. And then, all of a sudden, we swung around the handrail, rolled over the banister, and down the second-floor steps to the first-floor landing. When we hit the bottom step, I was lucky. My knee landed right on his nuts, putting him in a limp state. It gave me enough time to pick him up and push him out the first floor. When I did that, I slammed the door locking it behind him. He then started pounding on the door, yelling,

"Let me in!" I then yelled up the steps to Ronda,

"Call the police!" When he heard me yelling at Ronda about the police, it frightened him, and he left. Wow, it is finally over. I started walking back up the steps to Ronda's apartment. When I got to her door, I could hear her crying. She was a wreck, and she was sitting on the floor with her head down. I asked,

"Are you all right?"

I knew what just happened, but I thought we could continue talking and perhaps I could still get some. She looked up at me with tears in her eyes and said,

"Willie had no reason to do this." I now had a name to put with my attacker's face. So I walked over to her and tried to comfort her. I stroked her hair and said calmly,

"Relax, it's all over, everything is going to be alright." I know it was my hormones. I wanted to get her back in the same mood she was in before our little interruption. Then she said something to me that blew me away.

"Willie is crazy. He had no reason to do this, Jeff. Did you hurt him?" I didn't know much about women, but this confused me. So, of course, I answered,

"What?" And to my amazement, she repeated it,

"Jeff, did you hurt him?"

Well, to tell the truth, I hoped I would break his ribs, arm, and nuts, but I wasn't sure what I did to him. I didn't check him before I threw him out the door. But after a question like that, I could only reply,

"I think he's just peachy keen. By the way, I'm ok too."

That guy was trying to whip both our asses, and she wanted to know if he was alright. Now, that made me mad. What the hell was wrong with her? Ronda saw I was upset and decided to tell me her crazy scheme,

"Jeff I have to tell you the truth, I really wanted you to come to my house today, so I could make Willie jealous. But I had no idea that he would react that way. Please don't be mad, for real, I do like you, but I love Willie."

After she told me her plan. I wished I would have let Willie hit her. But all I wanted to do was get out of there. Ronda tried to cover up her mistake by saying,

"I'm sorry Jeff. Are you alright?" I felt like a fool and was very hurt. I wanted to cuss her out. But I just said,

"I'm out of here."

I turned and walked away. Walking down the steps of her apartment, I started taking inventory of myself. Well, my shirt and pants were torn, my arms were scratched up, my left shoulder hurt, both my knees were bruised, I had a lump on my head the size of a baseball, my lip was bleeding, and my left eye felt like it was swollen.

I have been in many karate fights, but I was never in one that caused this much damage to me. I didn't know anybody could be that insensitive. Still, I started remembering what Sensei said: See where you are. That meant I was in Ronda's apartment, a strange place. I should have been ready for anything. All I was worrying about was getting some.

Know who you are. I am a "man". I heard her say "last night," but I ignored it. And I had no real ties with her. I should have been more understanding of him and honored his request. All I did was let my hormones and stupid male pride get involved in my judgment. And, for real, I had no reason to defend her. Know what you are. I am a martial artist. All my practice and training were supposed to prepare me for that very moment. I took too many things for granted.

I thought about things for a while as I was walking home. On the way, I had to pass the Dojo. I saw the door open, so I went in. Sensei Lee was there training with a couple of other black belts I had never seen before. Sensei Lee took one look at me and said,

"That girl must have been a wild cat," one of the black belts heard Sensei Lee say the girl and said,

"Wow, a girl did all of that. The other laughed and commented,

"No means no." Then I explained to them what had happened to me. They looked like they understood my plight, but there was no compassion for me. I should have been more aware. Everyone was right, but I didn't think they would be so pitiless. That's when I made a mistake. I told them that karate doesn't work.

They all looked at me and asked me why I thought that way. So I explained what happened at the house. The old boyfriend came to the house. Then I told them I wasn't prepared for battle when the old boyfriend started yelling.

Then I told them I turned my back when the old boyfriend approached me. The two black belts looked at Sensei Lee and started to laugh and said,

"You're teaching him karate," embarrassed Sensei Lee looked at me and Said,

"Boy, before you say karate doesn't work, you have to do karate." Then he told me to go to the bathroom and clean myself up. Because I had just left Ronda's house, I didn't know what I looked like, so when I went into the bathroom and looked in the mirror, I was shocked.

You know the old saying, you look like you were in a fight. Well, I did look like I was in a fight. And all my assessments from before were correct, except for one thing. I didn't feel the long, bright purple scratch on my face running from the left side of my head to the left side of my chin.

It was very startling. I then cleaned the dry blood off my scars, tried to pull my tattered clothes back together, and went back into the Dojo. That was when I got the surprise of my life.

The three Sensei were standing in the front of the Dojo, all standing in a row. Sensei Lee, standing in the middle, said sternly,

"Mr. Washington I want you to leave this dojo, and don't come back till next Friday at six o'clock in the evening." The other black belt said,

"Practice hard, because when you return, we will test you for your black belt." Then the third black belt said,

"Do you understand?" I was shocked.

I just got in one of the worst fights of my life, and they want me to take my black belt test. Even though I was apprehensive, this is what I have been waiting for all my martial arts life. I was so surprised, I answered,

"Yes, sir!"

I turned and started to run to the door as fast as I could, and that's when it hit me. I didn't give the instructor respect.

I stopped, turned, and walked back to them like a little puppy with his tail between his legs. I stood before them and bowed. Embarrassed, and said,

"Sensei please forgive me for my lack of respect. That will never happen again." Sensei Lee replied,

"Make sure it doesn't." I then backed out of the Dojo, turned, and ran home. When I got home, I ran in the door yelling,

"Mom! Mom!" I was extremely excited about the test news, but I had forgotten entirely about my appearance. When my mother saw me, she put her hands on the sides of her face and yelled,

"My god, what happened to you!" I replied quickly to calm her,

"I was in a fight, but I'm ok. I got some great news." But for some reason, that did not calm her. She ignored what I said and replied compassionately,

"Who were you fighting, the united states marines?" I said again,

"Don't worry about how I look, I'm alright, I got news." My mother was always so caring when it came to me. She always told me she couldn't stand me in karate. She never wanted to see me hurt. I had been in many karate matches but had never been this damaged. So I had to make up a story to put her at ease, so I said brashly,

"Mom I fell off my bike, ok, now listen, I'm going for my black belt test next Friday!" My mother said, questioning about what I just said,

"You have to fall off your bike and hurt yourself to get a black belt test?" I could see my mother was only focused on my physical condition, so I just let it go and continued with my story,

"Mom I'm going for my black belt. What I have been wanting for years. I just have to be ready, so I'm going to practice." My mother was a little confused, so I just left the room.

I got up every morning and trained like never before for the next week. I did Punches, blocks, kicks, and all my katas whenever possible. I read books about karate and even books about other styles of martial arts. I didn't know what I would face, so I read the newspapers and magazines about fighting in any way.

I didn't leave anything to chance. I put all my heart and soul into my training. When the week was up, I was not only ready for my black belt test I believe I was ready for anything.

On the morning of the test, I got up anxiously and put on my uniform. The whole morning was a blur because I could only think about my test at six o'clock. I was so happy when my dad volunteered to drive me to my Dojo. It really fit into my plan.

The day dragged on, and I practiced until I thought I had it right. I looked at the clock, and I realized it was about five thirty, so I begged my dad to take me to my test early,

"Dad let's get going, I want to be there a little early," my dad reluctantly agreed and said,

"Boy, keep your shirt on you'll get there."

We got in the car when the worst thing I could ever imagine happened. My dad's car wouldn't start. I wanted to start cursing, but I didn't because if I did, my test would begin with my dad kicking my butt, so I calmly thought to myself, what was the next best option? Walk? I was about a half an hour away. If I start now, I can make it on time. So I thanked my dad, jumped out of the car, and proceeded to walk. While walking, I started to think, Am I going to be late? So I began to run. I ran about a half mile when I heard a familiar voice coming out of a car passing by.

"Hey guy need a ride?" of all the guys in the world, it could have been. I couldn't believe it was Greg, the first guy I was in karate with. He quit about seven years ago. I hadn't seen him for about two and a half years. He and his dad were riding by on their way to the store. I was so relieved I could hardly contain myself. Greg's dad rolled down the window and said,

"Do you want a ride?" I replied,

" Yes sir!" and I jumped in the car. Greg's dad said,

"Where to?" I answered,

"My karate school!"

And we were off. During the trip, Greg and his dad talked about many things, but I could not concentrate on anything they were saying; all I could think about was my test. When I saw the school, I wanted to jump out of the car while it was still moving, but I waited till the car came to a complete stop, then I leaped out of the car and yelled,

"Thanks!" and ran in the Dojo. Greg's dad asked Greg,

"What was he in such a hurry for?" Greg answered,

He is in a hurry to kick a board. They both laughed, and they drove away.

After all my worries, I was a little early, so I started stretching and went to the practice floor. As I entered, I saw three chairs, and in front of the chairs were some torn-up newspapers. I thought that was strange, but I didn't care; I was ready for the test. I stood there confidently, prepared to go. Then some anxiety started when I saw those three Sensei enter the room. They walked to the chairs and sat down. I didn't know why, but they didn't look happy when I looked at the Sensei's. That's when I decided to start. I approached the Sensei and stood at attention on top of the torn-up newspaper. I bowed and said,

"My name is Jeffery Washington, and I am here for my,: that's when Sensei Lee interrupted with a stern voice,

"How can you stand in garbage and talk to us!" I was so dumbfounded all I could say was,

"Black belt test."

I felt so stupid. I remember getting and giving pushups so many times for not keeping the Dojo clean. But because of my anxiousness, I forgot the dojo protocol. I leapt into action.

I quickly started picking up all the torn-up newspapers and dropping them into the trash can in the back of the Dojo. Then I ran back to the starting position in front of the Sensei's, ready to begin again. I'm not sure why, but that little prank calmed me down. I was determined not to let them trick me again.

So I waited for my instructions. And they came right away. They told me to do my punches, blocks, kicks, pushups, and sit-ups, and

I had to do all my Kata's. The Sensei tried the trick again by telling me to do one of my Kata's backwards. And I did it to perfection. I was in the zone. I felt so good that the Sensei all appeared to be pleased. So, they started the next phase of the test. Sparring, The Sensei's stopped the test and told me to rest. So I sat down, and I looked around.

All I could see were my hands and feet, which were bright red. My blood pressure was so high I could hear my heart beating. But I didn't care. All I wanted was my black belt. That's when the door opened, and ten guys walked into the room and stood in a row. I knew two of them but had never seen the others before. The guys I didn't know looked tough and were all bigger than me. I thought it looked like a tall mountain, so I had better get ready to climb it. The Sensei Lee called me over to the middle of the ring and said,

"Ready to start Jeff?" I shouted,

"I was born ready, sir!" He called the first guy over and matched us up. As you would know it, I didn't know him. All I thought was, It was on. I looked at my opponent, he was squeezing his fists and jumping up and down, staring at me with a mean look. That didn't worry me. It just made me mad that he was standing in the way of my black belt. Sensei Lee told us to bow to each other. We did. Then he grabbed both of our wrists and said,

"When I let go, start!" when Sensei Lee let go. In the blink of an eye, I delivered a perfect punch into my opponent's ribs. Then, I stood back and waited for Sensei Lee to confirm my point. Then all of a sudden, my opponent struck me back with two punches, one to my head and one to my ribs. I leaped out of the ring and yelled,

"Hey, Man! You hit me on the brake! What's wrong with you?" Sensei Lee ran over to me, stuck his finger in my chest, and yelled,

"What's wrong with him! The question is, what's wrong with you? You're in a fight, boy! You don't stop fighting till I tell you! Can you handle that!" Then he grabbed me and pushed me back in the ring and yelled,

"Now Fight!" For some reason, I was ready for this. It reminded me of the fight I was in about a week ago. But this time, the guy I was fighting didn't have a chair. Also, I wasn't going to turn my back on this guy. So, what Sensei Lee said was all I needed to hear.

Sensei Lee squared us up again. And we started. I threw an allotment of kicks and punches, all landing in my opponent's vital areas. My fighting skills pummeled my challenger down to the ground. I struck him so many times that he didn't even have the chance to hit me once. I was so precise all I heard was oohs and ahhs from the other Sensei's. Sensei Lee stepped in between us and stopped the fight when he looked like he had enough of my punishment. It all lasted about ten minutes. Then Sensei Lee called another guy into the ring. And he had a mean look on his face. I think he wanted to give me a good butt-whooping. And that pumped me up to fight harder. So, I got myself together and started to battle again. And it ended the same way, me knocking the guy I was fighting to the floor. And Sensei Lee stepped in and stopped the fight.

It was a little scary, but I focused on only one thing, I wanted that black belt. Man after man came into the ring, ready to defeat me. But all the fights ended with me being the victor. The fights went on for about an hour. And the more I fought, the more determined I was not to lose. I ended up fighting each guy about three times. That's when Sensei Lee wanted to see what I was made of. He sent two guys in the ring to fight me simultaneously. That concerned me for about a minute. Then, I managed to use it to my advantage. I started moving side to side, which confused my opponents and allowed me to get the better of them. After the ten were so bruised, they looked like they were hit by a car.

Sensei Lee was getting happier after every fight, but my opponents were not. They were tired of getting abused. That's when one of the black belts I was fighting had an idea. He walked up to me and whispered,

"Jeff, you're doing great. I think you passed. All you have to do is act like you're tired, and they will end your test." Even though I was doing well, for some reason, I didn't feel like I did enough. Then I started thinking about my journey. The exercises to strengthen my body, the fights in and out of the Dojo, the lessons that sharpened my mind about karate and life, the friendships that I had that helped me understand that I am not alone in the world, the sacrifices my family made for me helping get to this actual black belt test. I took a long, hard breath. And my Judges said,

"Stop!" The teachers in front of me instructed me to remove my brown belt, all smiling, saying,

"You have done well, we welcome you to be our next brother black belt," then they all bowed to me. Then Sensei Lee approached me and tied my black belt around my waist. Then, said,

"With rank comes responsibility."

I got my Black Belt. It's hard to believe it all started with a Professional Spalding Basketball, me believing in myself, and a Karate Guy.

The End

Japanese Terminology

Numbers

1.	Ichi	eech ee
2.	Ni	nee
3.	San	sahn
4.	Shi	shee
5.	Go	go
6.	Roku	roe koo
7.	Shichi	shee chee
8.	Hachi	hah chee
9.	Ku	koo
10.	Ju	joo

Japanese Terminology (Con't)

Commands

Dojo	Do jo	Place where you practice
Hajime	Hajee may	Start
Kata	Kah tah	Exercise
Kia	Kee yah	To yell
Kiatsoke	Kee aht soe kay	Attention
Sensei	Sain say	Teacher